Copyright © 2020 by Aggrandize Your Life Publishing, LLC.
All rights reserved.
Black Hair Love and Aggrandize Your Life, LLC, associated logos are trademarks and/or
registered trademarks of Aggrandize Your Life, LLC.

Library of Congress Control Number: 2020909530

Illustrations by Ija Charles
Edited by Armor of Hope Writing & Publishing Services, LLC
Editing team members: Destiny Nixon and Denise M. Walker
Layout design by Garry Atkinson, Fundo Press LLC
Logo design by Tenesha White, The New U

All rights reserved. No part of this publication may be reproduced in whole or in part, or stored in a retrieval system, or transmitted in any form, or by any means, electronic, mechanical, photocopying, recording, or otherwise, without written permission from the author. For information regarding permission, email aggrandizeyourlife@gmail.com

BLACK HAIR LOVE

by San Griffin

Featuring Illustrations by Ija Charles

DEDICATION

This book is dedicated to my late grandmother Mary, who looked forward to combing my hair when I came over on the weekends. Those were wonderful bonding moments I still hold dear. Also, to my father, Mr. Irving, thanks for teaching me how to braid, my first plait when I was a young girl. Additionally, to my late mother, Mrs. Pat, and my late maternal grandmother, Liz, thank you for always encouraging me to be creative. Finally, I dedicate this book to Morgan Elizabeth, my little cheerleader! Love you!

TABLE OF CONTENTS

Royal Spores _____ 1
Floret _____ 3
Beam On _____ 5
Radiate _____ 7
Head Wrap Favor _____ 8
Afro Admiration _____ 9
Beads Galore _____ 11
Young King _____ 13
You Are The Dream _____ 15
Woke Up Like This _____ 17
To Box or not to Box _____ 19
Sunday Night _____ 21
Truth Be Told _____ 23
Heroic _____ 25
Be Brave Be Smart _____ 27
New Seeds _____ 29
Art Credits _____ 31
About the Illustrator _____ 32
About the Author _____ 33
Special Acnowledgements ____ 34

ROYAL SPORES

Dear young girl or lad, when you look in the mirror

Don't be sad

You are a hero with your crown oozing through your pores

Every hair follicle is designed uniquely to create your

Natural royal spores.

Like an exotic bloom growing from the kiss of the sun,
Beaming with delight as water takes flight
Your beautiful hair is too, a natural unique flower
Growing straight up to kiss the sun.

BEAM ON

Hold your head up, don't look down

Have you ever seen a prince or a king with a bowed crown?

Let your confidence exude and beam straight through your hair

Just smile if they stare… perhaps you are shining so bright

They are having a hard time adjusting their pupils to the glorious sight

Don't dim your light!

RADIATE

COILS   CURLS   COILS

Moisturized with heavenly oils.
You were designed to receive,
Intercept the most intricate
Messages   from on
high,
smile with a sigh
Your antenna is built within,
For this you are sanguine!

HEAD WRAP FAVOR

Wrapped, twirled and zapped with love

My hair is protected like hands in a glove

Red, yellow or green, the colors

Not as important as the theme

AFRO ADMIRATION

"A" is for Afro
Afro Puff
Afro ponytail
Afro pom poms
Afro Mohawk
Thick, organic and regal
Yes, our hairdos are legal
Ancient, yet original
So perfect it's forgivable

BEADS GALORE

Oh, my beads

Forget over the rainbow

You are the rainbow

So bright, colorful with delight

Thread them on

Place them on

Rubber band in your hand

Lock them tight

That's right

Click n clack n' the sound of love we adore

The sound of beads galore!

YOUNG KING

My brother, my prince, growing king
You must master what self-control means
Observe Frederick Douglass, Jesse Owens and Dr. Charles Drew
They were pioneers, at best, who knew
Their hair was hard, strong and course
Like they had to be to help change this galaxy
You're one whether you have a twist-out, flat
Top or bald fade
Know you have a powerful lineage that was laid…

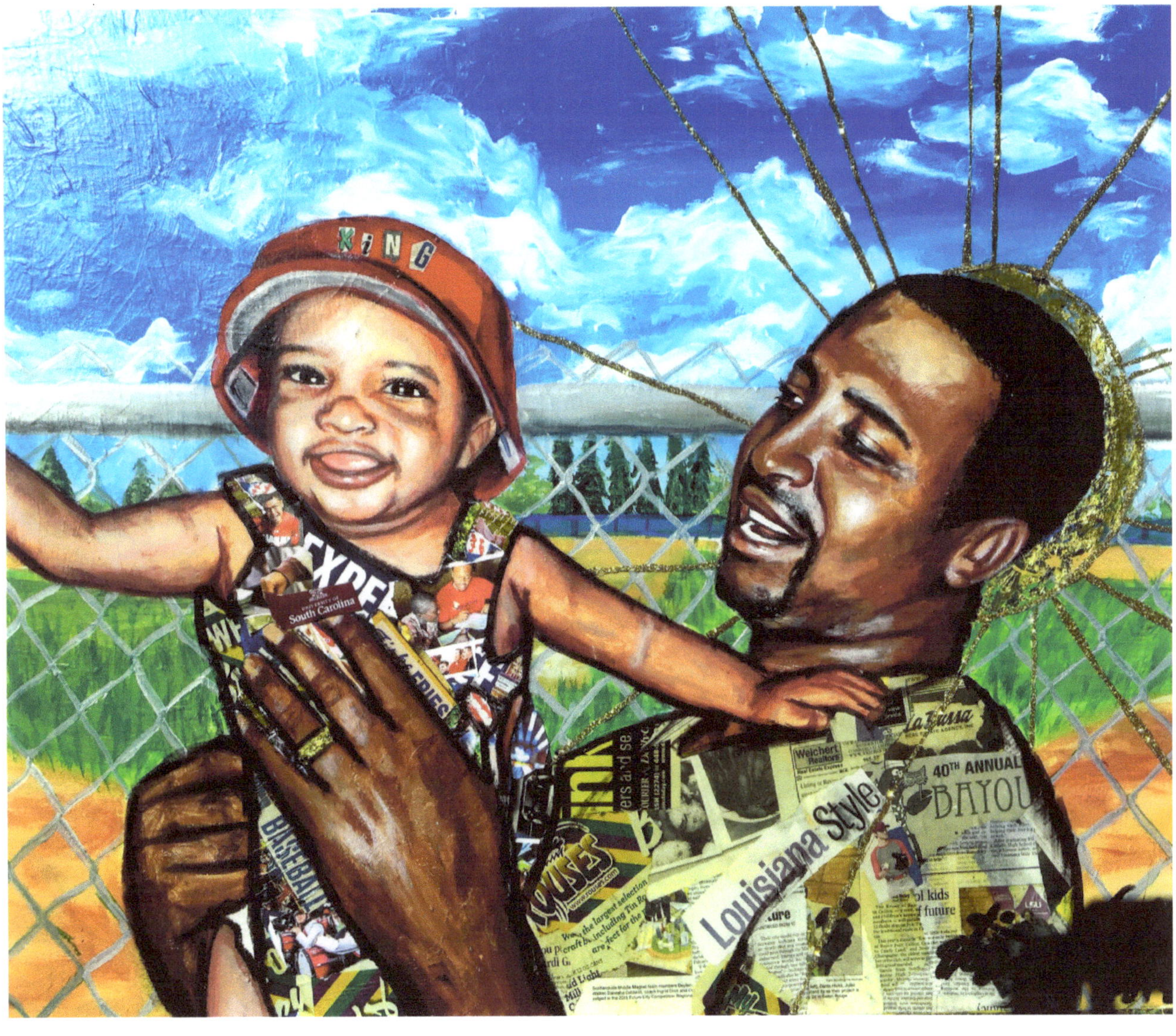
South Carolina
Weichert Realtors
40TH ANNUAL
BAYOU
Louisiana Style
ROUSES

YOU ARE THE DREAM

The tighter the knot
The closer the thought
Your genes are connected to the
Richest continent on the earth
Delicate minerals, gems, and natural
Resources flow in abundance
So does every follicle that oozes
Out of your rich pores on your head
Likewise, is a precious natural resource
Wear Africa's legacy with pride
Don't let other idle opinions override

WOKE UP LIKE THIS

Wake-up

Your hair standing straight-up on top of your head

A constant reminder it's not dead

A constant reminder you are a seed

Hair growing straight-up to the sun, not a weed

But like gladiolus, tulips, and sunflowers

A constant reminder you didn't come on the Mayflower

A constant reminder you are unique and you should adore

Every nook and cranny

Why?

Because you are beautifully and wonderfully made

Tell the naysayers, stop throwing shade

TO BOX OR NOT TO BOX

Don't fret, it's hard to conform and fit inside the box that other's built

People's wooden expectations can never tame your natural sentiments

When creativity exudes and oozes from your follicles

Actually, it's an organic flow as ancient as the pyramids and Kwanza River

SUNDAY NIGHT

It's Sunday night and momma's going to braid your hair tonight for the week

Wash, condition and moisturize, grease your scalp and watch the texture rise

Be still, hold your head up, look down, turn to the side, stop wiggling…

All the warm sentiments momma says

"Ouch," you exclaim,

When momma catches the edges we so affectionately call "the kitchen."

Yea our kitchen sometimes needs a little more love

It's part of our culture, our connection, our tradition.

Embrace these bonding moments for these are memories

Our ancestors and descendants will have in common

Put your silk scarf or bonnet on at night;

Keep the braids and cornrows looking tight.

Before you know it, it's Sunday night;

Now it's time to repeat that glorious exchange.

TRUTH BE TOLD

I have Indian in my blood, my hair runs red like

The mud in North Carolina dugs

Cherokee, Sioux or Navajo… maybe Coharie, Haliwa or Lumbee, no?

All so vital to U.S. History, their legacy is not a mystery.

Big curls, silky-straight, long locs-- jet black; it's all fine like Muscadines, rich in color

Jewels hanging, bedazzled, sparkling and fresh.

Sides dyed and laid to the side

Faded, cut high, cut low, suave and debonair, you know?

Gumby, flat top, retro look, and somethings you just can't find in a book

Passed down through culture, community and traditions

HEROIC

There is strength in my mane just like Samson and Dr. King!

Untold power that aligns every follicle

Love it

Nurture it

Maintain it

And it will reciprocate

Never desolate it,

Because there is strength in your mane

BE BRAVE BE SMART

Warm, thick, rich and dark as night
Your hair represents the strength of your fight
Fight for your goals
Fight for your peace
Fight for your foes
Each glimpse in the mirror of history
Reminds you, your strength is untold
Write your story, write it plain
Don't forget there's strength in your mane.

NEW SEEDS

Who said your hair is bad hair? Who planted those reckless seeds?

Words are seeds, indeed.

What you believe will proceed the truth, according to self-fulfilling prophecy

Plant the true seeds about your hair

Repeat it aloud and proud; you want it to reach the clouds:

My natural hair is magnificent just the way it is.

My hair is big like my giving heart.

My natural hair is thick and warm like the LOVE I share.

My hair is unique and dimensional like my bold personality.

My hair is coily like antennas that go straight up to the heavens.

My hair is strong like the strength of my ancestors.

My hair is versatile and resilient like me.

My hair is the result of my royal DNA.

My hair is marvelous and others do not define my hair.

I love all of me.

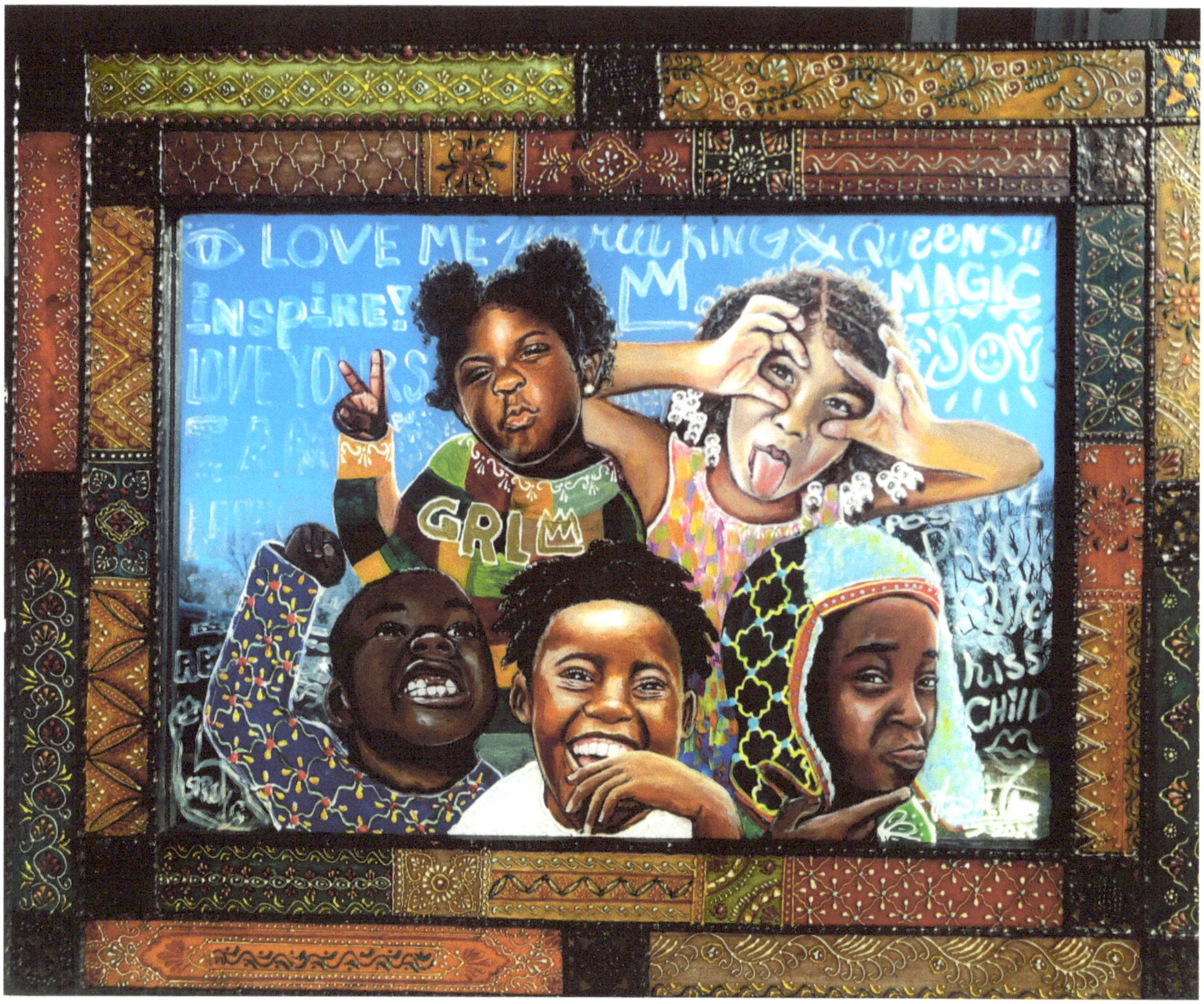
LOVE ME
INSPIRE!
MAGIC
JOY
GRL

ART CREDITS
CREATIONS BY IJA CHARLES

Page 2_____Untitled
Page 4_____You Don't Know Me
Page 6_____Free Your Mind
Page 10_____Sisters
Page 12_____OMG
Page 14_____Next Generation
Page 16_____Media Hustle
Page 18_____Boy Joy
Page 20_____Leap
Page 22_____Mothers Love
Page 24_____Blossom
Page 26_____Growth
Page 28_____Excellence
Page 30_____Sun Kissed Child
Page 32_____Ija Charles pictured with 'Sisters'

ABOUT THE ILLUSTRATOR

Columbia, South Carolina artist Ija Charles is a self-taught painter and entrepreneur. Her series range from portraits of ordinary people to a diverse sampling of symbols from our day to day culture. These images are then reimagined and reconstructed in her own unique way. Ija plants an idea for each new work and harvest the positive vibes her very foundation is based upon.

ABOUT THE AUTHOR

San Griffin, a skilled professional in child development and family relations, has worked with youth and their families for over 15 years. Black Hair Love is her second book, and first poetry anthology, which she plans to follow with more titles that empower, inspire, and powerfully impact readers of all ages. Her debut book is the Amazon bestseller, The Superheroes' Guide to Dominating Their Universe. As CEO of Aggrandize Your Life, LLC., her goal is to provide tangible and intangible transformative tools and resources through the literature and workshops she creates.

San earned both a bachelor's degree in child development and family relations, and a master's degree in human development from North Carolina Central University in Durham, N.C., where she lives with her husband, Milton, and three sons. Connect with her at www.aggrandizeyourlife.com

SPECIAL ACKNOWLEDGEMENTS

Thank you for reading and critiquing some of the poems, Aireaal and Erim. Tenesha, you are always supporting my vision, with amazing logos, thank you! Milton, my husband, who is my first beta tester, thanks for telling me this is something amazing, and believing in my skills even when I doubted myself. My friends and associates, Carolyn, Lashon and Anes, you ladies also read a poem or two and encouraged me to keep going. Thank you!

BLACK HAIR LOVE FANS,

visit

http://blackhairlove.redbubble.com

for merchandise!

BLACK HAIR LOVE

by San Griffin
Featuring Illustrations by Ija Charles

http://blackhairlove.info

www.ingramcontent.com/pod-product-compliance
Lightning Source LLC
Chambersburg PA
CBHW060809090426
42736CB00003B/213